Las Posadas

A Christmas Musical for Children
from the Mexican Tradition

Albert Zabel and Deborah Somuano

Production Guide and Teaching Ideas
by Debi Tyree

Abingdon Press
Nashville

Contents

LAS POSADAS

Copyright © 2007 by Abingdon Press

All rights reserved, except where specified. No part of this work may be reproduced or transmitted in any form or by any means, electronic or mechanical, including photocopying and recording, or by any information storage or retrieval system, except as may be expressly permitted by the 1976 Copyright Act or in writing from the publisher. Information about permission should be addressed in writing to The Copyright Company, 1025 16th Ave. South, Nashville, TN 37212.

This book is printed on recycled, acid-free paper.

Scripture quotations in this publication are from the New Revised Standard Version of the Bible, copyright © 1989 by the Division of Christian Education of the National Council of the Churches of Christ in the USA. All rights reserved.

ISBN 978-0-687-33498-5

Editor: Debi Tyree
Copy Editor: Julianne Eriksen
Designer: Steve Laughbaum
Cover Designe: Randall Butler
Cover Art: Bill Rose

07 08 09 10 11 12 13 14 15 16 — 10 9 8 7 6 5 4 3 2 1

MANUFACTURED IN THE UNITED STATES OF AMERICA

Synopsis of

Las Posadas

It's time for a children's choir to go caroling. But wait! Mrs. Romano, their choir director, is sick and cannot lead them. What will they do? Who will direct them? The children discover a note from Mrs. Romano encouraging them to go caroling under the supervision of Mrs. Morales, but Mrs. Morales quickly reminds them that she cannot direct the choir. The children decide they can do it! A caroler volunteers to direct. They try out one of their songs to make sure their idea will work ("Blessed Christmas Now Is Here"). As they carol, they visit a family decorating their home for Christmas. The carolers and the family share the Christmas story together and discover they have been learning a song that Mrs. Morales remembers from her childhood ("The Shepherds Go to Bethlehem"). With the help of the family, the carolers experience a bit of the tradition of Los Posadas ("Pidiendo Posada"). The musical ends with the cast and audience singing "Silent Night (Noche de Paz)" together. For groups desiring a time of cast member recognition, the option of singing "Reprise: Blessed Christmas Now Is Here" is included.

Cast List*
(in order of appearance)

Caroler 1	Mrs. Morales*
Caroler 2	Father*
Caroler 3	Mother*
Caroler 4	Child 1
Caroler 5 (opt.)	Child 2
Caroler 6 (opt.)	Joseph**
Caroler 7 (opt.)	Mary**
Caroler 8 (opt.)	Innkeeper**

Roles can be performed by children, youth, or adults. See "The Cast" on page 6 for flexible casting options.

*** Can be portrayed by any of the Carolers or Child 1 or 2. See "The Cast" on page 6 for options.*

The Music and Scenes

1. "Entrance Music" (Instrumental)
   Scene 1 (All Carolers, Mrs. Morales)

2. "Blessed Christmas Now Is Here" (Chorus)
   Scene 1 continued (Carolers 2, 3, 4, Mrs. Morales, optional Carolers 6 and 7)

3. "Transition Music" (Instrumental)
   Scene 2 (Father, Mother, Child 1 and 2, Mrs. Morales, all Carolers)

4. "The Shepherds Go to Bethlehem" (Chorus)
   Scene 2 continued (Mrs. Morales, Mother, Father, Carolers 1-4, Caroler 6 (optional), Child 1 and 2)

5. "Pidiendo Posada" (Joseph [outside singers], Mary, Innkeepers [inside singers], Chorus)
   Scene 2 continued (Father, Mother, Carolers 1-4, Child 1 and 2, optional Carolers 7 and 8)

6. "Silent Night!" (Chorus, optional solo; spoken: Father, Mother, Child 1 and 2, Carolers 1-3)
   Scene 6 (Miss James, Ashley, Jordan, Megan, Ethan)

7. "Reprise: Blessed Christmas Now Is Here" (Chorus)

Introduction to *Las Posadas*

Las Posadas combines three complementary elements—music, drama, and Bible study—to create an exciting Christian education experience for children ages 5-14. It includes all the information you need to produce and perform the musical. Las Posadas offers ideas to help leaders teach the story, the music, staging, and movement; and create sets, props, and costumes.

What You Can Do! (Reproducible!) (page 5)
- An overview of how to use the reproducible portions of this resource

The Cast (page 6)
- A complete cast list with options for small to large casts, tips on holding auditions and rehearsing a part

Rehearsal Organization (pages 7-8)
- Suggestions for organizing your rehearsal into sixty-minute or ninety-minute blocks, as well as producing a music camp!

Production Ideas (pages 9-11)
- Quick tips for producing the musical with simple ideas for movement, easy costume ideas, and options for sets (or even no sets!)

Las Posadas Snacks (pages 12-13)
- Quick, delicious, and fun theme snacks, including Fruity Quesedillas, Peanut Butter and Fruit Tacos, Mexican Hot Chocolate, Aguas Frescas, and a Healthy Piñata

Teaching the Music (pages 14-16)
- Warm-up suggestions, as well as tips for teaching the songs are included

Bible Story Helps (pages 17-19)
- A Scripture references, suggestions for telling the story, and crafts to reinforce the story

Julissa's Las Posadas Story (page 19)
- A personal story about the tradition of Las Posadas

More! (page 20)
- Several reproducible helps to make your production even more fun, including: Bulletin Cover (8½" x 11" folded), Casting Poster, Color Your Own Cover/Poster/T-shirt/Coloring Sheet, Word Games

Music Scores (pages 26-77)
- Includes a full vocal/piano score for the leader, melody/text edition for the singers, and instrument parts (all reproducible!).

Involving Other Ages

Enhance the intergenerational possibilities of *Las Posadas* by inviting other age groups to participate. Have youth or adults interested in dance create and teach the movements for the songs. Ask older children, youth, or adults to play the instrumental parts. Consider asking an adult who plays flute or recorder to play the second voice part. Encourage youth and adults to assist in various production-related activities. Perhaps they would be interested in being the helpers needed to serve in creating the sets or serving as costume manager, or stage manager.

The Sunday school and choir programs could produce this musical together by splitting responsibilities between a class, choir, or any combination that works best. Consider teaching the songs during Sunday school assembly time and have all the members of your Sunday school be the chorus.

Leadership Needed

Two primary leaders will most effectively provide leadership for *Las Posadas*. One leader could concentrate on learning activities related to the music, and the other could focus on the drama and production aspects of the musical. Recruit others to prepare the Bible story time and craft, snacks; make or assign costumes; help coordinate auditions, line rehearsals, choreography, and staging.

What You Can Do!
(Reproducible!)

Las Posadas is designed to allow total flexibility in producing the musical in your setting. Everything you need to produce the musical is included—the full score, singer's score, and split-track CD. You just need to add children, leaders, and a few props, costumes, or sets.

Adaptable!
- Need more spoken parts? Divide a part into two and create a new character! Remember that the parts are already partially divided for you with the use of four (or up to eight spoken parts) with the designation in the script of 1(4). (See *The Cast*, page 6 for more information.)
- Need *less* solos? Consider having all of the boys sing the Joseph solo and all of the girls sing the Innkeeper solos. Adjust the solos as best fits your group.
- Need *more* solos? Set aside stanzas or sections of a stanza of the chorus part as a solo, or have a soloist sing the second part to songs.
- Need a full set—create one!
- Have no need for a set—don't have one!
- Have projection capabilities? Project pictures to support the musical instead of using a set.
- Sing the musical in unison, or in two parts with an instrument or electric keyboard playing other parts. You could also ask a youth, soloist, or small ensemble to sing the second.
- All of the instrumental parts (C and B♭ instruments) are optional, but adding guitar (chords in the full score) and hand percussion, such as a tambourine, wind chimes, and guiro will enhance the performance. Use the CD as your guide for possible percussion and rhythm patterns. An electric keyboard can be used for the printed instrumental parts if desired.

Reproducible!
We know that it can sometimes seem confusing when we try to follow copyright laws and get permissions cleared. To make it easy for you to know what you can reproduce in this resource, items that are reproducible are marked as such with a "permission granted" statement. Please be certain to include that statement as a part of every page of your reproduction of the materials.
- Purchasers are given permission to reproduce a copy of the full score (piano/vocal score) for their accompanist(s).
- Purchasers are given permission to reproduce a copy of the singer's score (melody/text) for each of their singers and helpers.
- Purchasers are given permission to reproduce a copy of the instrumental parts for use by your instrumentalists.
- Purchasers are given permission to reproduce the CD to give to their singers to aid in learning the musical. You may not sell or charge a fee for the copies.
- Reproduction rights are granted to the original purchaser only and are not transferable. What does this mean? You cannot loan this score to another person to make copies for a production at another church. No one else has permission to make any copies—only the original purchaser is granted permission to make copies in their own setting.
- Purchase of this resource does not grant the right to sell or charge a fee for attendance to the performance, for videotapes of the performance, or for recordings of the performance. Contact The Copyright Company, 1025 16th Ave. South, Nashville, TN, 37212 (FAX: 615-321-1099) for information about permission in these instances.

The Cast

Minimum Cast: Nine persons (all children or combination of children, youth, and adults)

- Caroler 1: Significant number of lines
- Caroler 2: Significant number of lines
- Caroler 3: Significant number of lines
- Caroler 4: Significant number of lines
- Mrs. Morales: Child, youth, or adult female (very few lines)
- Mother: Child, youth, or adult female (moderate number of lines)
- Father: Child, youth or adult male (moderate number of lines)
- Child 1: Moderate number of lines
- Child 2: Moderate number of lines

Choirs Larger Than Six Members

The caroler lines have been divided for up to eight carolers. You will find the number for the lines for the four carolers listed first. The option of having up to eight carolers is designated by the number in the parenthesis. The designation "1(5)" means that it can be spoken by Caroler 1 OR by Caroler 5 in a larger cast. You may want to look closely at the amount of lines and memorization for each cast member and assign roles accordingly. If you have a choir of ten members, each child can portray one character. Choirs larger than ten may want to divide up some of the lines and create additional carolers. You may also discover that not all of the children would like a speaking part.

Holding Auditions

Invite all of the children to audition for a part or solo; you never know what skills or talents a child may have to share. You may also want to send a note to the children's parents confirming the date of the auditions, the rehearsal and performance dates, and a reminder that you will need their help in practicing and memorizing lines at home.

Review the script and have in mind the kind of personality needed for each character. You will need to decide if you would prefer to have the children try out for a specific part or solo or to have all children try out on the same lines or solo verse. Talk with each child about their desires and share with them that you will cast the musical keeping in mind each person's interests and strengths.

- Dramatic roles: Select a passage for each child to read. Listen for inflection. Create a familiar situation for determining ability to pantomime. For example, ask the child to respond to a surprise birthday party, a loud, startling noise, a funny joke, and so forth.
- Solos: Select a stanza for each child to sing. Let them sing it two times for you to help them overcome any nerves about singing in an audition.

Rehearsing Lines

Know how you want speaking parts to be delivered and work toward this end. Model for the children the image of the characters you have in mind, but allow for personal interpretation as well. As you talk with the children about their characters, emphasize that development of the character is just as important as learning the lines or basic movement. Ask the children to practice their roles with one another at home, over the phone, in front of a mirror, and so forth. Encourage them to listen and watch one another during rehearsals with other characters. It is often helpful for some children to have a set deadline to have completed memorization of their part. Consider dividing the musical into smaller sections and set dates by which to have memorized their part for that section.

Rehearsal Organization

How long will it take to learn this musical? That depends on several factors in your setting. Consider how many children will be participating. What is the average age of the children? Are they primarily readers or nonreaders? Do you have several adults who are willing to undertake strong leadership roles such as musical director, drama leader, movement leader, and so on? Are you producing this as a part of your regular children's choir ministry or as a music camp?

If you will be rehearsing this over several weeks, and your group is primarily comprised of younger children/beginning readers, consider holding more rehearsals that are sixty minutes in length. Plan to spend no more than approximately ten minutes on any game, song, or activity. With groups primarily comprised of children who read or older elementary age children, or in settings where you can partner a younger child with an older child, you may want to consider the ninety-minute rehearsal plan.

Suggestions for rehearsal organization are given for a sixty-minute rehearsal, a ninety-minute rehearsal, and a two- and three-hour music camp. You may need to adjust the timing slightly for your group and rehearsal setting. You may also discover that you need to switch some of the elements in the schedule; for instance, snack time may fit better earlier (or later) in your setting.

Consider introducing the songs one by one to the children from the very first rehearsal of your choir year. Intersperse the Bible story studies throughout the fall. As you come near to the end of October, begin planning for movement and drama rehearsals during your regular choir rehearsal schedule. Plan to spend more and more of your rehearsal time on the production of the musical as you near the performance date.

SIXTY-MINUTE REHEARSAL

Ten Minutes
- ❑ Gathering and Welcome
- ❑ Warm-up

Thirty Minutes
- ❑ Music Rehearsal

Fifteen Minutes
- ❑ Drama/movement/Bible story (*Alternate each session as desired.*)

Five Minutes
- ❑ Announcements
- ❑ Closing prayer
- ❑ Say "Good-bye!"

NINETY-MINUTE REHEARSAL

Fifteen Minutes
- ❑ Gathering and welcome
- ❑ Vocal/mental warm-up
- ❑ Overview

Thirty Minutes
- ❑ Music rehearsal

Twenty Minutes
- ❑ Drama, movement, and/or Bible story (*Alternate between sessions or divide the time frame between two topics.*)

Ten Minutes
- ❑ Snacks/refreshments

Fifteen Minutes
- ❑ Review a Song from the Musical
- ❑ Announcements, Question and Answer Time
- ❑ Closing Prayer
- ❑ Say "Good-bye!"

THREE-HOUR MUSIC CAMP

Twenty Minutes
- ❑ Gathering and Welcome
- ❑ Devotion and Prayers
- ❑ Vocal/Mental Warm-up
- ❑ Overview/Focus for the Session

Thirty Minutes
- ❑ Music rehearsal

Thirty Minutes
- ❑ Drama/Movement Rehearsal

Twenty Minutes
- ❏ Snack and Recreation

Twenty Minutes
- ❏ Bible Story

Twenty Minutes
- ❏ Crafts, Games, or Free Play. *(Consider using this time for solo rehearsals, blocking for lead characters, line rehearsals, or for extra rehearsal on songs.eded.)*

Thirty Minutes
- ❏ Music Rehearsal *(Move to production rehearsals midway through the music camp.)*

Ten Minutes
- ❏ Announcements, Question/Answer Time
- ❏ Closing Prayer
- ❏ Say "Good-bye!"

Do you want to include very young children in your production of Las Posadas?

- Create rebus (picture) charts for the verses. Songs such as "Blessed Christmas Now Is Here" can be easily taught using these charts. (Use this in worship as an anthem as well!)

- Use lots of silly movements as you teach the song. Dance around the room singing the same phrase or verse over and over—make a game out of it!

- Make sure each child has a copy of the music CD. This age group learns very quickly by listening to music as they participate in other activities at home and riding in the car.

- Send the Singer's Book home with the children. This will serve as a quick reference for mom or dad when trying to figure out a text after a CD listening session.

- Set shorter goals for this age group and when they achieve the goal make a BIG deal out of it! Instead of having a goal of the entire song memorized by then of a rehearsal, go for just the first twenty measures of text or a single verse. Create a chart that has many goal spots between starting to learn the song and "memorized."

- Be creative! If your very youngest choir can only handle singing the first song (and certainly a stanza of "Silent Night"), adapt the script slightly to make it seem as though you have two choirs going caroling. One choir (the younger children) goes offstage with their parent helpers while the other continues with the story. At the end the younger choir can "knock on the door" and join the older group in the home to sing "Silent Night."

- Young children need very specific placement on stage. Use small pieces of painters (low tack) tape on the floor to help them remember where to put their toes.

- If you have a very wide age group, consider creating staged "family" groups, with an older child serving as the caregiver for a very young child.

Production Ideas

Costumes

Carolers and Child 1 and 2 should wear play clothes appropriate for Christmas in your community. Do you have a church or community T-shirt? Perhaps the caroling cast could wear that shirt! Is it cold in your area in December? Wear outer clothing as appropriate. Mrs. Morales, Father, and Mother can wear clothes that are typical of your community.

You may want to add simple pieces of cloth as headpieces to the children portraying the roles of Joseph, Mary, and the Innkeeper. Traditionally, Mary and Joseph would be in full biblical costume. The addition of a tunic, headdress, or a simple handheld prop, such as a candle, will add to your production. These should stored in the box that is on stage that is marked Christmas Decorations and Costumes.

Sets and Props

The production of *Las Posadas* does not require a set to be effective. Here are some ideas of sets and props. Invite church members to help you create these and encourage them to be creative in developing the sets and props.

SIMPLE SET—SCENE 1: Borrow a small table for Scene 1, add a "note" from Mrs. Romano. Perhaps add a music stand or a few rhythm instruments. If you have a portable chalkboard or white board, you could draw a staff with a variety of musical notations on it, including "rehearsal schedule" and so on. Place it to the side of your performance area. Or place it on a lower level than the set for Scene 2, such as on a lower section of a chancel area.

FULL SET—SCENE 1: Add a painted backdrop of a choir room! Create a "wall" with a window. Add some painted-on music posters of famous quotes or even a large music staff as if you were looking at a chalkboard or whiteboard with a staff on it. Include all of the items from the Simple Set—Scene 1.

SIMPLE SET—SCENE 2: A chair, a side table with a Bible and a battery operated candle on it, a partially decorated Christmas tree, a large Nativity prominently displayed, and a large cardboard box or plastic tub clearly marked "Christmas Decorations." In the box you will need:

1. Several tree ornaments — for Mother and the children to hang at the beginning of Scene 2.

2. Several lengths of colored tree garland — for doorways for Joseph and the Innkeepers.

Ask two children to hold the garland as if it was a doorframe. Each child will hold the garland to create one of the ìtop cornersî of a doorframe. This will allow approximately three feet of garland between the children with five to six feet of garland left to hang down as the sides of the doorframes. Decide how many sets of doorways you have space (and children!) for and then purchase the garland. Choose all of one color or mix the colors—it's your choice!

3. Costumes for Joseph, Mary, and the Innkeepers. You can choose between costuming only a single child as Joseph, Mary, and the Innkeeper or several children or all of the children.

A broom laid near the Christmas Decoration Box could become Joseph's staff and Mary should hold the candle found on the table. Simple headpieces can be made from large squares of material and inexpensive stretchy headbands. These will pop on very quickly. If more of a costume is desired long tunics or vests could be put over the children's play clothes. All of the children in the cast would have fun putting on the simple headdresses. Choose any square of scrap fabric that may be available, but make the scraps large enough to hang between the children's shoulder and waists when made into a headdress. Consider making the squares out of a Christmas fabric and giving them to the children to take home after the production to use as a Christmas table covering in their home.

4. Figures from the Nativity set — Mary, Joseph, baby Jesus, angels, shepherds and animls if available.

FULL SET—SCENE 2: Add a painted backdrop of thehome. Include a wall with family pictures, perhaps a window with a curtain or fireplace, Christmas garlands, and other typical decorations you would find in a home. Add another chair and table (you could place the Nativity set on the second table), plus all of the items listed in the Simple Set—Scene 2.

Staging the Musical

You will need to consider the space in which you are performing *Las Posadas* before beginning to block (place the cast in specific places) the musical. Issues to consider are placement of microphones, the width and sight line of your performance area, availability of a curtain (stage) or no curtain (a chancel area.) Microphones usually set the area of most of the action. Work with the person who will be helping with the sound equipment to decide the best placement for the microphones. All the blocking will be defined by the placement of the mics.

1. Entrance Music: Plan the entrance of the carolers and Mrs. Morales so that they are in the performance area by the end of this music. A few stragglers may want to come in on the first lines depending on your space. Group the children in interesting groups of two and three, mixing heights as you can. Repeat the music as needed.

SCENE 1: The children should move to the microphones in groups and speak as if in a conversation. Place the children so all can be seen. Help them turn their bodies on a diagonal line so their bodies are facing the person they are speaking to, but their faces are facing the mics. For instance, Carolers 1-4 could be blocked to stand together until the note is found. At the end of the scene the children should stand in a line/s as if they were performing a song in choir.

2. Blessed Christmas Now Is Here: See movement suggestions below.

3. Transition Music: The cast exits the stage area. Consider several ways of having the cast re-enter in Scene 2—perhaps down the center aisle or from another doorway.

SCENE 2: The scene begins with the Mother and the children decorating the tree. Father enters as soon as "3. Entrance Music" is finished. The carolers should begin singing soon after they hear the Child 2 line. Depending on where the carolers are placed, they may have to sing very softly! Practice the timing of their entrance so they reach the area of the home on Father's line. Mother can mime opening the door so the carolers can enter. Block the full cast the way a caroling group enters a home—they tend to stand close together around the edges of an area of a room. Father should sit down in the chair. That will allow the various characters to move to the mics as needed. Father should pick up the Bible to read the scripture lesson. The children may be blocked to stand beside him, kneel beside the chair, or stand behind the chair looking over his shoulder as they read. They could also pass the Bible to one another—or a combination of these movements! Children who are not reading could place the figures into the Nativity scene as the story is read. (If you choose not to do this, then place the figures into the Nativity instead of the decoration box.)

4. The Shepherds Go to Bethlehem: See movement suggestions below.

SCENE 2 CONTINUED: At the end of this scene Mother should hand out props and costumes to the children. If you have a large number of children to be costumed, Mrs. Morales, and Father can help also. Give the garland to the "door frame" children, and costumes to Mary, Joseph, and the Innkeeper first so they can be moving into place as the other children put on their costumes. You have twelve measures of introduction to "Pideindo Posada" to get into place as well.

5. Pidiendo Posada: See movement suggestion below.

SCENE 2 COMPLETED: The cast should move back to their places from the beginning of Scene 2. Leave on the biblical costumes through the end of the musical

6. Silent Night: See movement suggestions below.

7. Reprise: Blessed Christmas Now Is Here: See movement suggestions below.

Movement

You may want to add simple movements to several of the songs in the musical. One of the children or a youth may want to help develop the movements for you. Remind them to keep the movements simple and keyed to a beat or a specific word in the text to help everyone move in unison. Here are some simple movement suggestions for the some of the songs:

2. Blessed Christmas Now Is Here. Use a few words in sign language to add motion to the music of measures 13-20 and 38 to the end.

Go (vamos): Lift both hands up to your shoulders pointing with your pointer fingers. Swing them forward, moving one after the other.

Bethlehem (Belén): There are three movements for this word: (1) Move the thumb of your right hand across your palm, with the other fingers standing straight up and together (creating the sign for the letter "B"). Hold your hand palm out in the area of your shoulder; (2) Move your hands to the left at your chest, touch the top of your fingers together creating an inverted V with your hands. Gently tap the tops of your fingers once on the left side of your chest, and then; (3) tap once on the right side of your chest. This tapping works well on beats 1 and 2 on the half note of the word Belén.

Jesus: Tap the middle finger of each hand into the palm of the other hand as if touching the wounds in Jesus' hands

Manger: Create V's with your pointer and middle fingers (think peace sign) and intertwine them by placing the middle finger of one hand into the V of the other hand to create a "manger." You may want to consider asking the children to slowly move the îmangerî forward as they sing the next phrase.

Free: Begin by touching your pointer fingers to your thumbs (creating small circles on each hand, the sign for the letter "F"). Cross your arms at your chest, palms facing in. In a smooth motion, move your arms apart and until your hands are up at your shoulders, palms facing out (fingers still touching).

4. The Shepherds Go to Bethlehem: You will want to add rhythm instruments to this piece as noted in "Teaching the Music." If you decide to have the whole cast do simple movement, keep them very simple to allow the children to focus on singing the text. Consider asking two to six of your more talented dancers to create a special dance for this song. The rest of the cast can focus on singing! You may want to create a simple motion for the words "tam" and "bou" to have fun on the repetitive word sections. Also consider creating a simple motion that each part could do as they sing their part to visually create the back and forth pattern. Simple movements could include a side step touch dance pattern over eight beats in one direction and then reversing directions for eight beats (measures 5-8, 6-12). On measures 13-15, switch to simple forward toe taps (one touch forward and then back for each measure, alternating feet). That sets you up for your fun motion for the rest of the stanza. On stanza 2 you may want to ask one child to portray the role of the little shepherd boy who mimes falling down and crying until the "Ay, Ay" text begins the toe tap patterns.

5. Pidiendo Posada: You will want to keep movement to a minimum except during the interludes between the stanzas. The interludes represent the time of moving to the next home to find shelter. Depending on your space consider the following.

- Asking Mary and Joseph to move in a large circle around the performance area during the interlude ending at the next doorway. There is an optional repeat written in to allow for the time to do this as needed.

- Creating a walking movement for the whole cast—step in place to the beat for three measures, stop and raise hands to your eyes as if looking for one measure, and then repeat this pattern as desired.

- During the four sets of the interlude you may combine several ideas to create visual interest (and to help the children remember what to sing when!). Do a different movement each time. Ask the instrumentalists to stroll across the stage one time (guitars, percussion, and melody instruments). Perhaps Father, Mother, and Mrs. Morales could do the step–look pattern by themselves one time. Be creative!

6. Silent Night: Las Posadas experiences often include candles. Many churches include candle lighting as a part of their Christmas celebration. You may want to consider the best way to safely incorporate candles into your performance during the singing of "Silent Night." Purchase battery-operated candles for your cast! Watch for sales and coupons at craft stores during the month of December.

Using battery-operated candles will allow you total flexibility in movement. For instance, hold the candles at waist level on stanza 1, swaying left to right on beat 1 of each measure. Consider asking the children to slowly move the candles up on stanza 2 (or create a candle choreography that is more intricate), and on stanza 3 consider dimming the stage lights so the candles glow brightly, or moving children so that a star shape with streamers is formed by their candlelight.

Las Posadas Snacks

These snacks are designed to be quick and easy to serve as a rehearsal time snack. You may also want to explore more options that will give your experience an authentic Mexican flavor. Consider asking participating families to bring a food from Mexico for a party after the performance.

- A quick search on the internet will bring you hundreds of authentic recipes for foods such as Flan, Mexican Wedding Cookies, or Three Milk Cake. Ask church members who love to cook to provide an authentic dessert at each of your rehearsals. Serve the children's favorite dessert after the performance.
- Purchase a cookbook that features Mexican foods and share it with your church cooks. Consider having a Mexican dinner as a part of your performance. After all, Las Posadas always involves family, friends, fellowship, and FOOD!
- Visit a local Hispanic grocery store for ideas of tasty foods to serve. A local Mexican bakery will offer lots of tempting sweets for you to purchase.
- Stroll through the Hispanic food section of a local grocery store. You will find prepackaged snacks for your children to try.

Fruity Quesadillas
(Makes 8 servings, ½ quesadillas each)

½ cup sour cream
¼ tsp. vanilla extract
⅛ tsp. sugar
Variety of fruits, peeled, diced or sliced into
    small ¼ inch pieces (pears, strawberries,
    grapes, mangos, apples, and so on)
1¼ tsp. honey
1 cup shredded cheddar cheese
1 tsp. finely chopped fresh mint
4 eight-inch flour tortillas

Mix together the sour cream, vanilla, and sugar. Chill in the refrigerator. Warm the honey slightly in the microwave and toss gently with the fruit and the mint. Spread half of each tortilla with the shredded cheese (reserve half of the cheese). Strain any liquid from the fruit mixture and divide the fruit mixture among the tortillas. Top with the remaining cheese and fold each tortilla closed. Spray a skillet with cooking spray and preheat to a medium temperature. Grill the quesadillas until brown. Prior to serving, cut each quesadilla in half and serve with the sweetened sour cream.

Peanut Butter and Fruit Tacos
(Makes 1 serving; multiply as needed. The children can make their own taco if there is time.)

1 flour tortilla
2 tbs. peanut butter
½ cup strawberries (hulled and sliced)
¼ small can crushed pineapple, well drained
½ sliced banana
¼ cup coconut flakes

Spread the peanut butter on the tortilla, add sliced banana, strawberries, pineapple, and coconut. Fold in half and eat! (Consider variations of the fruit choices depending on what is available in your area.)

Mexican Hot Chocolate
(You can find powdered mix in some grocery stores, but making this from scratch is delicious and easy.)

Per serving:
1 cup milk
½ disk of Mexican chocolate or
    2 oz. dark bitter chocolate
½ vanilla bean split lengthwise

Warm the milk and chocolate together in a pan. Scrape the seeds from the vanilla bean(s) and add both the seeds and the bean to the milk mixture. Whisk until melted and the mixture just begins to boil. Remove from the heat and whisk the chocolate milk until it froths. Serve immediately.

Aguas Frescas

(A favorite drink sold by street vendors and cantinas in Mexico. You will also find this in some grocery stores as a prepackaged mix, but it is so easy to make fresh, why not involve the children?)

Wash and cut into 1-inch pieces any ripe fruit, such as pineapple, cantaloupe, strawberry, papaya, or watermelon. Blend the fruit until smooth. Add water until the mixture is thinned to a very light color. You may need to strain the mixture to remove any fruit pulp or seeds. Sweeten to taste with sugar or sugar substitute. The drink should be the consistency of water. The proportion is approximately 2 cups fruit to 3-4 cups water, but you will need to experiment to come to the perfect taste with your fruit. Add a dash of fresh lime juice to add pop to the mixture! Chill well before serving (or blend the fruit and water with ice to chill the mixture as you create it.)

Healthy Piñata

Purchased empty piñata
Prepackaged portions of fruit-chews, fruit
    rollups, pretzels, small crackers, and so on

Stuff the piñata with the snacks. Many piñatas come with ribbon pulls that allow the children to take turns choosing a ribbon to pull, rather than hitting it with a stick (much safer for the children and the building)! If you do use a piñata that requires a stick, ensure that the children and others are far away from the child attempting to hit the piñata.

Teaching the Music

Use Your Voice!

The most effective tool to use to teach a new melody is your voice. Sing a phrase of a song to the children. Ask them to sing the phrase back to you. Tap a hand drum to keep a consistent beat. Make a game out of seeing how many phrases they can learn and sing back to you correctly. If you need help, ask the accompanist to play the melody line only as they sing. This will help the children focus on matching pitch, rhythm, text, and phrasing. You will be surprised how quickly they will learn the phrases! This technique is called "lining out" a song. When you can, make a game out of learning the music. Ask the children, "Can you sing four phrases correctly?" or "Can group 1 count how many "t's" group 2 sings together?"

Consider your choir members and decide if you will be singing the second parts. All of the second parts are optional. Other ideas include asking a youth to sing the part, having a C instrument play the part, or teaching short repetitive sections of the second part to the whole choir or even a small group within the choir.

The teaching suggestions given are designed to be used over several music sessions. For instance, when using the suggestions for "Blessed Christmas Now Is Here" you may want to use the first bullet point at the first session and the next bullet point as a part of the next rehearsal, and so on. Teach a variety of songs during each rehearsal to keep the children interested and engaged in the rehearsal.

Vocal Warm-Ups

Use a variety of warm-ups to prepare the children for rehearsal. Include slow melodic phrases, phrases that uses a limited number of intervals of thirds, fourths, and fifths, and text combinations that encourage crisp articulation and enunciation. Always encourage the use of head voice when the children are singing.

Consider these fragments from *Las Posadas* for use as a warm-up:

2. Blessed Christmas Now Is Here
- Measures 16, beats 3-20: Work on articulation, rhythm, and mental focus.

5. Pidiendo Posada
- Stanza 8, measures 91-94: *Legato* phrasing, vocal range (move up and down by half steps).

4. The Shepherds Go to Bethlehem
- Create a body band for mental and rhythmic focus.
- Write these three melody line rhythms on three different pieces of posterboard.
  1. Measure 5: Tap the rhythm on your knees or fingers.
  2. Measure 18: Snap or clap the rhythm.
  3. Measure 6: Slide palms of hands together to the rhythm.
- Teach each of the parts using the charts, switch parts between small groups of children.

Teaching Suggestions

Since many of the children will already know the tune to "Silent Night," you have only three new songs to teach. Use simple games, posters and charts, and the Listening CD to help the children learn the texts.

2. Blessed Christmas Now Is Here
- Line out the first phrase (measures 4-8) on *loo,* asking the children to repeat the phrase.
- Line out the second phrase (measure 8, beats 3-12) in the same way. Ask if they are the same or different? (Different) How are they different? (The end of the second phrase starts a little higher and moves down.)
- Sing measures 4-12 using the text of stanza 1. Line out measure 12, beats 3-16 and then sing these measures using the text. Ask them to join you in singing this whole section. Tell them you are going to sing the last phrase. Ask, "Have you heard this music before?" (Yes!) Ask them to join you in singing the first stanza. Note that the pronunciation guide and translation for the short phrase in Spanish is at the bottom of the music score.
- Create sentence strips to help memorizing the text. Purchase or create sentence strips out of posterboard. Write each phrase of the text on a

strip. Jumble the phrases together and see how fast the children can help get the text in the right order. Use the first phrase from each stanza as a memory "jogger" as the children begin to memorize the text.

- Ask the children to help you discover the order (form) of the song by naming the sections. Consider using letters or shapes on small pieces of posterboard to help them visualize the form (♥ – ♥ – ♥ – ▲).
- Help them find measure 42 in the music. Sing the ending together. Discuss where the music is the same and where it is different from what they have sung before. Show them your symbol for that section (▲).
- Decide how you will be singing the second part. Share this with the choir and begin adding the second part once the children are confident in singing the melody. You may want to consider teaching the second part on the short phrase that is sung in Spanish to all the children (as on the recording). Make a game out of singing the parts. Divide the choir into two parts and practice having each group sing the parts. You may need to ask a youth or another leader to help lead one group as you help lead the other group as they sing the parts together. Continue playing the game of singing together and switching parts until the choir can sing the parts together confidently.
- Review sections of this song at each rehearsal until the choir can sing the song from memory.

4. The Shepherds Go to Bethlehem
- Tap out the rhythm of measures 5-8 on a hand drum. (If you don't have a hand drum, a large, empty plastic coffee can works well.) Say the text to these measures, encouraging the children to join you. Hint: Use this drum tap as a transition moment throughout your rehearsal.
- Line out the four-measure melody, tapping as you sing. Repeat this pattern until the children can sing it confidently. Ask the children to open their music and find this song. Ask them to look at the music notes of measures 5-8 and 9-12. Are they the same or different? (Same.) Sing this section from each of the stanzas.
- The first eight measures of each stanza of this song would work well for soloists. Perhaps you have children or youth singing who could sing a duet. Even hesitant singers could sing these eight measures as a solo or in a small ensemble. Let the children know if you will be having soloists sing these phrases.
- Play the Listening CD of this song. Ask them to raise their hands when they hear a part they

recognize. Encourage them to open their music and sing the phrases with the CD. (Work separately with soloists and ask them to sing it with the choir as soon as they can.)
- Divide the choir into the two groups that will be singing the call and response sections at the end of each stanza. Ask them to find measure 13, and remind them of their part. Sing this section to them, asking them to raise their hands when they hear their part. Ask them to join you in singing this section. (For a fun tension reliever, ask them to stand and then quickly sit down when they sing their part.) Review measures that may need a little more work on the pitch or text.
- Consider adding rhythm instruments, such as tambourine and castanets. Depending on the skill of the players, improvise simple patterns to play throughout or simply on measures 16-22 and 37-43. Hand drums, guiros, tambourines, and castanets will add the percussion to make this piece come alive. Build the instrument parts so that each stanza has a different sound.
- Review sections of this song at each rehearsal until the choir can sing the song from memory.

5. Pidiendo Posada [*Pee-dee-YEN-doh Poh-SAH-dah*]
Share with the children that this song expresses what might have been said between Joseph and the Innkeeper. Depending on the size of your choir, there are several options for performing this song.
- Joseph and the Innkeeper sections can be sung by different children as solos on each stanza. They would each stand in a "doorway."
- Joseph solos could be sung by one child with different children standing at each doorway as singing Innkeepers, creating a small ensemble of Innkeepers (as recorded).
- Half of your choir could sing the Joseph stanzas and the other half sing the Innkeeper stanzas. Consider staging the two groups of children on different sides of the performance area. Actors miming the roles of Joseph and the Innkeeper would move from doorway to doorway.
- Use and combination of the above! If you are combining these options, start with a soloist and move to larger ensemble combinations as the song progresses. Note that everyone but Joseph sings stanzas 8 and 10. Everyone in the cast sings stanza 12.
- Line out each section of stanza 10 on "*loo*," emphasizing the *legato* movement of the melody and the first beat of each measure.

- Share with the children that this song is comprised of five sets of conversations between Joseph and the Innkeeper, with the final set sung between Joseph and the entire cast. Ask them to listen (or sing along) to the CD, standing when it is their part in the conversation. After listening to the entire song ask, "Which stanza had a new melody?" (stanza 12).
- Line out stanza 12, singing on *"loo,"* or playing the melody on the recorder, piano, or flute.
- Create simple word help charts on posterboard. Combine the first few words of the paired stanzas on each piece. This will help the children learn the groupings of the stanzas.

1. In the name of heaven	9. Here I am
2. This is not an inn	10. Are you Joseph

- Play memory games as suggested in other songs to learn the text. Cut apart your posters and ask each "side" to hold up their stanza help as they sing—can they do this in the correct order? Make a game out of which side can hold up their correct text most often.
- Review sections of this song at each rehearsal until the choir can sing the song from memory.
- In the traditional text, the name "Queen of Heaven" is used for Mary. It is retained for historical reasons. You may choose to use "blessed Mary" instead.

6. Silent Night! (*Noche de paz!*)

Don't presume that all of the children know this song. Ask the children to hum the melody as you play it on the recorder, flute, or piano. Work on moving together with exact rhythms and on open vowel sounds and crisp consonants. Remind the children that they will be singing this as a choir, not just singing along with a congregation.

- Consider singing the first stanza in Spanish. Ask someone in your community who is fluent in Spanish to come and lead the children in learning the pronunciation of the first stanza in Spanish.
- Speak the text in rhythm until everyone can speak the text comfortably. Say it in the tempo that you will be singing this song. Use the rhythm of the melody as you speak. Play simple games to make the repetition fun, such as tossing a bean bag and asking the child who catches the bean bag to say the next phrase. Gradually move so that there is no loss of tempo as they speak. Collect or purchase inexpensive plastic disposable cups. Give each child a cup and ask the children to kneel in a circle. Turn the cups upside down and practice moving the cup to sit in front of the person on your right—all at one time. Tap a slow beat and move the cups several times. Set a slow tempo and ask the children to say the text as they pass the cups around. See how long you can go before someone loses their cup or loses the beat. Tap a drum to help them set a constant tempo.
- Review sections of this song at each rehearsal until the choir can sing the song from memory.

Pronunciation Guide

NOH-cheh deh pahs,
NOH-cheh deh ah-MOHR
TOH-doh doo-EHR-meh ehn deh-rreh-DOHR.
EHN-treh lohs AHS-trohs keh ehs-PAHR-seh
   soo loos BEHyah,
ah-noohn-see-AHN-doh ahl nee-NYEE-toh
   heh-SOOS.
BREE-yah lah ays-TREH-yah deh pahs,
BREE-yah lah ays-TREH-yah deh pahs.

---

7. Reprise: Blessed Christmas Now Is Here

- The children have learned this song already! Ask the children to open their music to this song and look at the music. Ask, "Have you sung this song before?" (Yes. It's part of the first song.)
- Sing it together!

Bible Story Helps

Luke 2:1-20

House of David

Scripture: Luke 2:1-5
- Invite a volunteer to come dressed in a Bible costume. The volunteer should portray the role of the person sent to read the decree from Emperor Augustus. They may want to have a scroll that has Luke 2:1-3 written on it. Ask a child to finish the reading (Luke 2: 4-5.)

Discussion Starters
- What do you know about your family history? What is the country of origin for your family? When your parents or family talk about "going home to visit," where do they mean?
- What do you think Mary and Joseph took with them on their trip?
- Why was it important that Jesus be born in the city of David called Bethlehem?

Craft: Get Registered
- Materials: A large piece of posterboard with several columns on it. Consider including "name of pet," "type of pet," "number of pets," and so on to the posterboard. Decorate the posterboard as desired to give it the look of an official document. You will need a marker to write on the posterboard.
- How-to: Ask the volunteer dressed in the Bible costume to sit at a table with the poster and marker. The volunteer should announce: "Emperor Augustus has declared that a registration must be taken and you are to participate." Invite each child to stand and tell them what kind of pet they have and how many pets are in their house. You may want to ask information about the pet's name, color, and so on depending on how much time you have. The volunteer should mark on the posterboard the information given by the children. After all the children have spoken, help them tally the total number of pets they have registered.

Craft: Registration Pen
- Materials: Ballpoint pens, variety of colored pony beads, white "tacky" glue, cord/twine, several small disposable bowls, baby wipes.

- How-to: Cut an eight-inch piece of cord for each child. Pour white glue into small bowls. Tie a knot in the end of a piece of cord and string beads onto the cord. Leaving approximately three inches of cord, knot the other end of the cord. Dip the longer loose end of the cord into the glue and wrap around the top (not the writing end) of the pen, smoothing as you go. Set aside to dry. Clean up messy fingers with the baby wipes.

No Place for Them in the Inn

Scripture: Luke 2:6-7
- This portion of the scripture coordinates with the celebration of Las Posadas. Read the short story, "Julissa's Las Posadas Story" (page 19). You may also share from one of the resources under "Las Posadas Resources" (page 00) .
- Sing "Pidiendo Posada."

Discussion Starters:
- What reasons could the Innkeeper have for not giving Joseph and Mary a room in the inn?
- The Bible doesn't tell us what was said between Joseph and the Innkeeper. If you were writing a song about this scripture lesson, what would you say to Joseph?
- Is the fact that there was no room in the inn the most important part of this scripture? What is?

Craft: Welcome Door Signs (Older Children)
- Materials: Several 5" x 7" pieces of cardboard/tag board/posterboard. Hole punch, ribbon, stickers, markers, glitter glue, odds and ends of trims, sequins, and so on. You will need at least one permanent marker. (You can also purchase foam door hangers.)
- How-to: Tell the children, "We are going to make a sign for our doors so visitors will know they are welcome." Help the children to write WELCOME in large letters on their sign with the permanent marker. Encourage the children to creatively decorate the signs with the craft supplies.

Craft: Swaddled Fingers! (Young Children)
- Materials: Washable marker, a 12" x 1" strip of natural muslin (one per child).
- How-to: Ask each child to put out their left pointer finger, palms up. With the washable marker, draw two dots and a mouth on the top of their finger (creating the baby's face.) Wrap the cloth around the rest of the finger tying it loosely at the base of the finger ("swaddling the baby"). Place the "baby" into the palm of your right hand and curve the right hand to make a manger. Reread the scripture and ask the children to raise their pointer finger "babies" at the beginning of verse 7, and to place the baby in the manger when you read "and laid him in a manger."

Shepherds and Angels

Scripture: Luke 2:8-14
- Mime the story! Collect several swatches of cloth and fabric strips for shepherd headpieces (and perhaps a stuffed sheep or two). Wired garland wrapped into a halo will work for the angels. Pass out the costumes and ask the children to react as their character as you read. Switch costumes so that each child has a chance to be both a shepherd and an angel.

Discussion starters:
- Why did you react as you did when you were a shepherd (angel)?
- Why did God make sure the shepherds in the fields knew about the birth of Jesus?

Craft: Glory! Mobile
- Materials: Wired garland (cut to 18" lengths for each student), variety of colors of curling ribbon, markers, scissors, cardstock paper, hole punch.
- How-to: Twist the garland into a circle, twisting ends around the garland to secure. Cut six freehand shapes out of the cardstock. (For a more uniform mobile, consider creating an angel stencil for the shape.) Using a marker, write one word of the phrase "Glory to God in the highest" on both sides of each shape. Confirm that each child has written each word of the phrase on the card shapes before moving to the next step. Help each child punch a hole on one end of the shapes. Tie the shapes to the garland circle using differing lengths of ribbon. Curl extra pieces of ribbon and tie on as decoration. Use another piece of ribbon to create a hanger for the mobile.

Let's Go to Bethlehem

Scripture: Luke 2:15-18
- Using large letters, write "Let's go!" "There they are!" "You won't believe what we saw!" and "Wahoo God!" on different pieces of paper. Ask two youth or adults to practice reading the story and lifting a sign. The cues are:
  - ❑ Verse 15*b* (Let us go now to Bethlehem)—"Let's go!"
  - ❑ Verse 16 (and found Mary and Joseph)—"There they are!"
  - ❑ Verse 17 (they made known what had been told them about this child)—"You won't believe what we saw!"
  - ❑ Verse 20 (shepherds returned)—"Let's go!"
  - ❑ Verse 20 (praising God)—"Wahoo God!"

Before reading the scripture, practice raising the signs and asking the children to read them loudly and enthusiastically. Remind them to do that each time the signs are held up as the scripture is read.

Discussion Starters:
- Pretend you are one of the shepherds. What would you tell Mary and Joseph? Why do you think people were amazed at what they heard? (verse 17)
- Read verse 19 again. What do the words *treasured* and *pondered* mean in this setting? Why do you think Mary both treasured *and* pondered the shepherd's stories?
- Why do you think the shepherds returned to their fields glorifying and praising God?

Craft: Praise God! Picture
- Materials: Cast picture, posterboard, markers, a permanent marker, variety of sequins, small beads, miniature ornaments and other small decorative objects, inexpensive acrylic frames to match the size of the picture.
- Using the markers and posterboard, make a poster of the text, "Praise God for all you have heard!" Have a cast picture taken in front of your set. Make sure your poster can be read, that all of the cast can be seen, and that there is some "background" on the outside edges of the picture. Print one copy for each child.
- How-to: Insert the picture into a frame. Glue on the sequins and other small pieces to fill in the space or highlights along the edges of the background. Allow to dry completely. Write each child's name on the back of their frame with the permanent marker.

Julissa's Las Posadas Story

I can barely control my excitement! My aunt is coming from Mexico to visit us for Las Posadas. Everyone in my family has been working together to prepare for it. Today, when I got home from school, the smells coming from the kitchen were fabulous. I ran into the kitchen and asked my mother, "Is she here yet?" I must have asked that question one too many times over the last few days because my mother just rolled her eyes at me and kept on making tamales.

I have been celebrating Las Posadas forever, or so it seems to me. When you look in our family picture albums, there are pictures of our family gathered in our kitchen cooking, at my grandmother's house decorating, or at one of the parties. At some point or another, my brothers and sister have played a part in Las Posadas. This year is my year! I am going to play the part of Mary on the eighth night of Las Posadas!

My name is Julissa and I am eleven years old. My heritage is Mexican. My grandparents live in my neighborhood, but many of my relatives live in other cities in Mexico and the United States. By now you are wondering, "What is Las Posadas?" In my excitement I forgot to tell you all about it!

Las Posadas has been celebrated for a very long time, expecially in Mexico. Las Posadas is Spanish for "the inns." During the nine days of Las Posadas, we learn of Mary and Joseph's journey to Bethlehem when Jesus was due to be born. On the nights of December 16 and December 24, my family attends a church service. Then we travel to church members' homes. Sometimes the homes are close to the church and we all walk together, singing carols all the way. Other times, everyone piles into several cars or the church bus to go to the homes. It is a great honor to be one of the host homes. Some people light the way to the homes with candles set inside paper bags and weighted down with sand. Have you ever seen those?

Each night of Las Posadas we act out the story of Mary and Joseph trying to find a roon in an inn in Bethlehem. A few persons gather inside the host's home to play the part of the innkeepers. Everyone else stands outside the home to play the part of the peregrinos or pilgrims. Each night, Mary and Joseph take their place at the door of the home. Mary and Joseph are played by a girl and a boy dressed in costumes from Bible times. We all stand behind Mary and Joseph, ready to come into the home—if Mary and Joseph are invited to enter! Mary and Joseph knock on the door. As the innkeeper opens the door, we sing a song. The song alternates between the pilgrims asking for shelter for the night and the innkeepers complaining about being bothered by the weary travelers. The song goes back and forth between the two groups many, many times. Finally, the innkeepers invite everyone to come in. Everyone, pilgrims and innkeepers alike, sings a final stanza together, giving thanks that the baby Jesus is to be born. Then the party, with food, prayers, and lots of carol singing, begins!

It is important for me to celebrate Las Posadas because it prepares me for Christmas. My family can't always attend every night of the celebration, but we try to go to church as many nights as we can. Even when we can't attend the parties, we spend time together making food, singing carols, and telling the Christmas story over and over. The tradition of Las Posadas reminds me that the true meaning of Christmas is that Christ the Savior was born!

Wait! I hear someone coming in the front door! My mother smiles and shakes her head "yes" as I ask once more, "Is she here?" My aunt is here! She brings the costume that she and my mother wore when they were young girls portraying Mary in Las Posadas. This year I will be wearing the costume! I hope that you will be able to find a celebration of Las Posadas in your community. Look closely—maybe the girl playing Mary will be me!

More! (Reproducible)

We have included several more reproducible items to make your production of Las Posadas even more fun!

Bulletin Cover
- Use this to create a cover for your program.

Casting Poster
- Make a copy of this page and add the names of your actors. Post this Casting Poster so they will know who will be portraying what role in the musical.

Color Your Own Cover
- Copy and use this as a fun coloring sheet or as a poster. Add specific information on the back (time, date, place) about your performance and use it as an invitation. Glue the colored sheet to a larger piece of posterboard and add the time, place, and date of your performance to create a publicity poster. Create T-shirts using special transfer papers and paints or fabric crayons. Visit your local craft store to explore the possibilities.

Word Games
- Use these as early arrival activities, craft, or take home sheets to help in the learning of the musical.

Las Posadas

A Christmas Musical for Children from the Mexican Tradition

Albert Zabel and Deborah Somuano

Las Posadas

A Christmas Musical for Children
from the Mexican Tradition

Albert Zabel & Deborah Somuano

——— T H E   C A S T ———

Caroler 1: . . . .
Caroler 2: . . . .
Caroler 3: . . . .
Caroler 4: . . . .
Caroler 5: . . . .
Caroler 6: . . . .
Caroler 7: . . . .
Caroler 8: . . . .

Mother: . . . .
Father: . . . .
Mrs. Morales: . . . .
Child 1: . . . .
Child 2: . . . .

Soloists: . . . .
Joseph: . . . .
Innkeeper: . . . .

Other: . . . .
Other: . . . .

Create Your Own Cover!

Provide the children with highlighter markers in several bright colors. Have them use the markers to add color to the picture below.

Word Games

Copy this page and cut the games into three separate games to be used individually as you teach each song.

Jumbled Blessed Christmas Now Is Here

Oh my! The verses are all jumbled up! Circle the phrases that are in the wrong place or verse!

1. We sing praises, we sing praises, give our hearts unto the child.
   We rejoice now, for the child has come to us, we rejoice now.

2. We will give him, we will give him, blessed Christmas now is here.
   We will find him, we will love him, our sure hope and life is there.

3. We will love him, we will find him for the lesson that he brings
   He, the richest poor became. We will praise him, we will praise him.

The Shepherds Go to Bethlehem — Fill in the Blank

How well do you know the words? Fill in the missing words. Tip: Sing the song to yourself as you work and you'll have them figured out in no time!

1. Rushing ___ to Bethlehem, shepherds are _____ torn up shoes in _____, clothing all aflutter. Ay, ay, ay, we cheerful __, Ay, ay, ay, we'll ____ return. Sing _ tam, tam, tam, and a bou, bou, bou, ____ a tam ___ a bou, as the tambourine _____, and ___ castanets.

2. ____ a little _____ boy fell down on the ____, and the others ____ to him, "Stay, we _____ wait!" Ay, ay, __, we _____ go, Ay, ay, ay, _____ soon return. ____ a tam, tam, ___, and a bou, ___, bou, sing a tam and a bou, as ___ tambourine plays, ___ the castanets.

3. Jesus we ____ sing to you, _____ growing weary; _____ of God, now _____ you cry, for we'll love ___ ever. __, ay, ay, __ cheerful go, Ay, ay, ay, we'll soon _____. Sing a ___, tam, tam, and a bou, bou, ___, sing _ tam and a ___, as the _____ plays, and the _____.

Pidendo Posada — Match Up

Match the first phrase of each petition from Joseph with its matching answer by the innkeeper by drawing a connecting line between them!

Joseph	Innkeepers
In the name of heaven hear me	Go away from here, go now
Listen, oh dear innkeeper	This is not an inn, my good man
Here I am, good innkeeper	We don't know a man named Joseph
Do not be so cruel to us	If she is the queen of heaven
In the name of heaven hear me	Are you Joseph, man of Naz'reth

1. Entrance Music

(Keyboard, opt. B♭ or C Instruments)

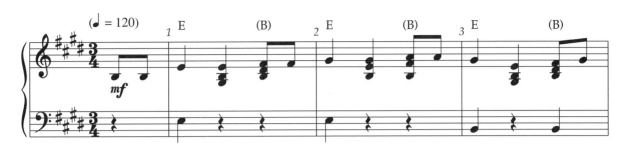

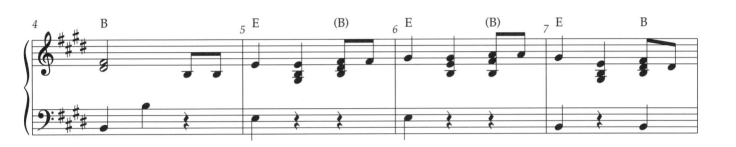

*(Several **Carolers** and **Mrs. Morales** enter.)*

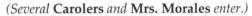

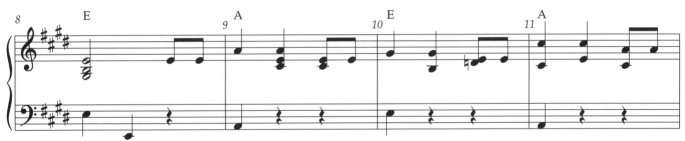

Repeat as needed.

MUSIC: Trad. Argentina, arr. by Albert Zabel

Scene 1

*(Several **Carolers** and **Mrs. Morales** enter during Entrance Music.)*

Caroler 1:   Come on everyone. Let's get ourselves organized.

Caroler 2:   Do we have to go caroling when it's so cold?

Caroler 3:   Of course we do. Don't be so wimpy. We'll have a good time.

Caroler 4:   I wonder where Mrs. Romano is. We can't do our singing without a director.

Caroler 1 (6):   She must be running late.

Caroler 3 (7):   Look! There's a note on the table. *(Looks at it.)* It's from Mrs. Romano.

Caroler 1 (5):   Let me read it.

Caroler 2 (6):   *(Picks up note.)* I've got it.

Caroler 3 (7):   I found it, please let me read it.

(The note is handed to Caroler 3 [7] who reads the note while Caroler 2 [6] reads over their shoulder.)

Caroler 3 (7):   "Dear Children, I'm not feeling very well today. I won't be able to go caroling with you."

Caroler 4 (8):   *(Interrupting)* Oh no, that's bad news.

Caroler 3 (7):   *(Continuing to read.)* "Mrs. Morales will go caroling with you. Love, Mrs. Romano."

Caroler 2 (6):   Wait! There's more. "P.S. Be sure you practice the new Spanish carol before you leave."

Caroler 1:   But we can't practice without a director!

Caroler 3:   Mrs. Morales? Could you direct us?

Mrs. Morales: *(Sadly shakes her head "no.")* I don't know how to direct a choir.

Caroler 4:   What are we going to do?

Caroler 1 (5):   We still need a leader. How can we practice without a director?

Caroler 2:   I can do it. I can direct.

Caroler 4 (8):   No way!

Caroler 2:   Yes I can!

Caroler 4 (8):   This will be a disaster.

Caroler 3 (7):   At least let *him/her* try. That's what Mrs. Romano would want.

Caroler 1 (5):   Well, since you put it that way. I guess something is better than nothing.

Caroler 2:   Okay. Now everybody sing out, and watch me.

*(**Carolers** line up to sing as if in rehearsal.)*

2. Blessed Christmas Now Is Here

(Keyboard, opt. B♭ and C Instruments)

Pronunciation: vah-mos vah-mos ah es-pae-rahr-lo, vah-mos vah-mos ah bay-lin
Translation: Let's go, let's go wait for him, let's go to Bethlehem

WORDS: Trad. Argentina, trans. by Deborah Somuano
MUSIC: Trad. Argentina, arr. by Albert Zabel

(mel. is top note)

praise him, we will praise him, He, the rich-est, poor be-came. *Va-mos va-mos a es-pe-*

(mel. is bottom note)

rar - lo, va-mos va - mos a Be - lén. Our Lord Je - sus, in the man - ger, came to

set all peo-ple free, came to set all peo-ple

free, came to set all peo-ple free.

Caroler 2: Not bad. In fact, pretty good, if I do say so myself. I think I like this job.

Caroler 4: Don't get too excited. Remember, you're only a substitute.

Caroler 3: Come on. Stop fussing.

Caroler 1: I think we can do it!

Caroler 3 (7): Mrs. Morales, I'm glad you'll be with us.

Mrs. Morales: I'm glad to help out. I loved that song you were singing. I remember hearing my mother sing it.

Caroler 2 (6): Did you live in Mexico?

Mrs. Morales: Years ago when I was a child. Well, are you ready to go?

Caroler 2: We're ready. But, don't forget to watch me when we sing!

(Exit as the "Transition Music" plays.)

3. Transition Music
(Keyboard, B♭ or C Instruments)

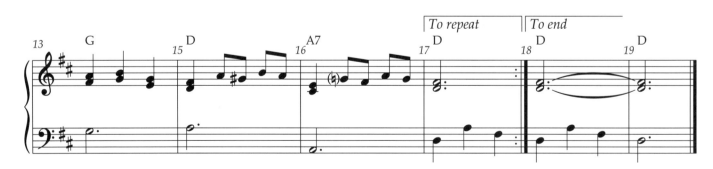

MUSIC: Traditional, arr. by Albert Zabel

Scene 2

*(The scene opens on a living room with **Mother** and **Children** finishing decorating a Christmas tree. A Nativity set is prominently displayed. **Father** enters from the outside.)*

Father: Here are the rest of the decorations. Is it ever cold outside! And that wind—it chilled me to the bone.

Mother: Here, have something warm to drink. Remember those Christmases we had in Mexico? We never saw a bit of snow.

Child 1: I'll bet it wasn't very cold.

Child 2: I'm glad it's nice and warm in here.

Father: You're lucky you're not outside. Here, let me help you with that ornament.

Child 1: I can do it myself!

Father: Aren't you independent! You know, sometimes we do have to let others help us.

Child 2: May I put on the star?

*(**Carolers** are heard singing "Blessed Christmas Now Is Here" from offstage.)*

Mother: Of course. I think we're about done. Isn't it a pretty tree?

Father: Listen! There are some carolers outside. I saw them coming downt the street when I was outside.

*(**Children** look out the window.)*

Mother: Isn't that wonderful! Let's invite them in. They must be cold.

Child 1: No. Don't ask them in. They're strangers. We don't know them.

Child 2: I don't think they're from around here. They might be dangerous.

Child 1: Or different.

Father: Don't be silly. Where's your Christmas spirit? Mother, let them in.

*(**Mother** opens the door.)*

Mother: Come in! Come in! I'm sure you'd like to get out of the cold for a few minutes.

*(**Carolers** enter.)*

Father: Your singing was wonderful.

Caroler 4: We've been practicing very hard.

Caroler 2: Our director is very sick and couldn't come with us. I had to be the substitute director.

Mother: You're doing a fine job.

Caroler 1: My mother came along to help out.

Mrs. Morales: Good evening. I'm Anna Morales. Thank you for letting us come in. That cold is really wicked and we've come a long way.

Mother: You're most welcome. Please make yourself at home.

Father: We just finished decorating our tree and I was about to read the Christmas story from the Bible. It's something we do every year.

Mother: Come join around our manger scene.

Child 1: May I help read?

Child 2: Me, too?

Father: Of course. Perhaps some of our guests would like to read also. But let me begin. "In those days Caesar Augustus issued a decree that a census should be taken of the entire Roman world. This was the first census that took place while Quirinius was governor of Syria. And everyone went to his own town to register."

Child 1: "So Joseph also went up from the town of Nazareth in Galilee to Judea, to Bethlehem, the town of David, because he belonged to the house and line of David. He went there to register with Mary, who was pledged to be married to him and was expecting a child."

Child 2: "While they were there, the time came for the baby to be born, and she gave birth to her firstborn, a son. She wrapped him in cloths and placed him in a manger, because there was no room for them in the inn."

Caroler 1 (5): "And there were shepherds living out in the fields nearby, keeping watch over their flocks at night. An angel of the Lord appeared to them, and the glory of the Lord shown around them, and they were terrified."

Caroler 4 (8): "But the angel said to them, 'Do not be afraid. I bring you good news of great joy that will be for all the people. Today in the town of David a Savior has been born to you; he is Christ the Lord. This will be a sign to you: You will find a baby wrapped in cloths and lying in a manger'."

Child 2: "Suddenly a great company of the heavenly host appeared with the angel, praising God and saying, 'Glory to God in the highest, and on earth, peace to men on whom his favor rests'."

Caroler 3 (4): "When the angels had left them and gone into heaven, the shepherds said to one anther, 'Let's go to Bethlehem and see this thing that has happened, which the Lord has told us about'."

Mrs. Morales: It's such a beautiful story.

Caroler 1: I really love the part about the shepherds.

Mrs. Morales: It reminds me of that carol I heard you practicing last week.

Caroler 3: I know the one you mean. It's about the little shepherd that fell down and was left behind.

Mrs. Morales: That's it! Would you sing it for us? I remember it from my childhood.

4. The Shepherds Go to Bethlehem

(Keyboard, B♭ or C Instruments)

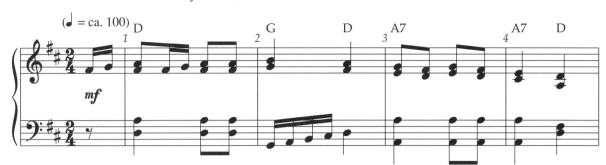

*1. Rush - ing off to Beth - le - hem, shep - herds are wear - ing
2. Then a lit - tle shep - herd boy fell down on the road, ___

torn up shoes in tat - ters, cloth - ing all a - flut - ter.
and the oth - ers said to him, "Stay, we can - not wait." ___

*Optional: Soloist can sing stanza 1 and/or 2.

WORDS: Traditional, trans. by Deborah Somuano
MUSIC: Traditional, arr. by Albert Zabel

© 2007 Abingdon Press, admin. by The Copyright Co., Nashville, TN 37212

Mrs. Morales:	Thank you so much. That's such a happy piece and always one of my favorites.
Mother:	Let's finish the Bible story.
Caroler 2 (6):	"So they hurried off and found Mary and Joseph, and the baby, who was lying in the manger. When they had seen him, they spread the word concerning what had been told them about this child, and all who heard it were amazed at what the shepherds said to them."
Father:	"But Mary treasured up all these things and pondered them in her heart."
Child 1:	"The shepherds returned, glorifying and praising God for all the things they had heard and seen, which were just as they had been told."
Father:	What a wonderful story. I hope all of you will treasure it in your hearts as Mary did.
Mother:	Do you know, when we were your age, we lived in Mexico. At each year we had a celebration at Christmas called Las Posadas.
Caroler 1:	Las Posadas?
Caroler 3:	What was it about?
Mother:	It was about a part of the Christmas story you just heard.
Caroler 4:	About the shepherds?
Caroler 2:	Or the angels?
Father:	No. Remember what happened when Mary and Joseph reached Bethlehem?
Child 1:	The baby was coming at any moment.
Child 2:	And they couldn't find a place to stay.
Father:	Right! Las Posadas tells the story of Joseph looking for a place where the baby could be born. Remember the story says, "there was no room for them in the inn." Inns are what we might call hotels today. I imagine they went to several of them, but they were always turned away.
Mother:	No one would even open the door for them.
Child 2:	Maybe they were afraid because Mary and Joseph came from another town.
Child 1:	They were strangers.
Child 2:	That's why we were a little afraid to let all of you in.
Father:	I have an idea. I think we should celebrate our own Posada. We have enough people here.
All:	Really?
Father:	Sure. Let's set up some inns—here, here, and over there. Some of you can be innkeepers and two of you can be Mary and Joseph looking for a place to stay.

(**Children** divide into groups. **Mother** hands them props to create doorways.)

Father:	Are you ready? Now there's a little tune we sing as we go from place to place. It's very easy and we can all join in. Innkeepers, take your places. Mary and Joseph ready? Okay. Here we go.

5. Pidiendo Posada

(Keyboard, B♭ or C Instruments)

First time: Joseph (O)
Second time: Innkeepers (I)

1. In ____ the name ____ of heav - en ____
2. This ____ is not ____ an inn, my _____

hear me, I ____ must plead ____ with you for _____ lodg - ing.
good man, You ____ must keep ____ on search - ing _____ this night.

WORDS: Traditional, trans. by Deborah Somuano
MUSIC: Traditional, arr. by Albert Zabel

© 2007 Abingdon Press, admin. by The Copyright Co., Nashville, TN 37212

40

First time: Joseph (O)
Second time: Choir and Innkeepers (I)

7. Lis - ten, oh ___ dear inn - keep - er, I ___ now
8. If ___ she is ___ the queen of ___ heav - en, who ___ seeks

ask ___ for lodg - ing ___ with you. I ___ need on - ly
lodg - ing from us ___ this night, why ___ does she ___ come

shel - tered in our house. _____

Father:	So, at last Mary and Joseph found a place to stay.			
Mother:	A place where the precious baby could be born safely.			
Caroler 1:	It probably wasn't anything fancy.			
Caroler 2:	They may have been as cold as we were when we came in.			
Father:	Perhaps. But, what's the important lesson we can learn from the Las Posadas drama we just did?			
Caroler 3:	I know. Never give up.			
Caroler 4:	Or, keep on trying.			
Mother:	Good ideas, but I think there's a lesson even more important.			
Child 1:	Sometimes it's okay not to be afraid of strangers.			
Child 2:	Sometimes strangers need help.			
Caroler 3 (7):	And strangers can become neighbors and friends.			
Mother:	Can anyone remember a Bible verse about neighbors?			
Caroler 4 (8):	I know. Love your neighbor as yourself.			
Father:	Good for you! Jesus taught us that everyone is our neighbor. Everyone is to be loved—even strangers.			
Mother:	In the book of Matthew, Jesus says, "I was a stranger and you took me in."			
Caroler 3:	Just like the last innkeeper took in Mary and Joseph.			
Father:	That's called hospitality. It comes from the same word as hospital—a place where people are cared for and welcomed. It also means sharing the gifts that God has given us.			
Mother:	I like to think back to that first Christmas so many years ago. It was such a silent and holy night. The most wonderful night that ever was.			

6. Silent Night!
¡Noche de paz!

(Keyboard, B♭ or C Instruments)

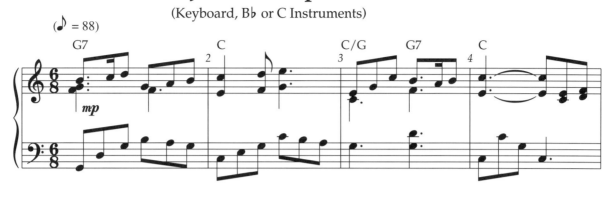

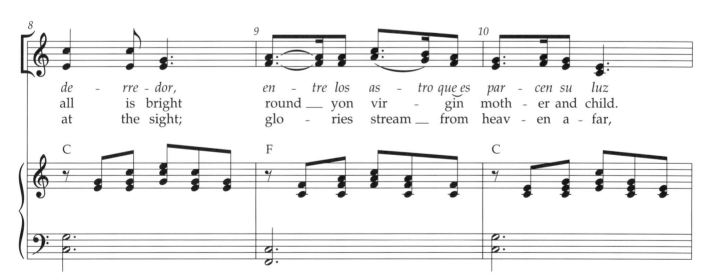

Options: The choir may sing the Spanish text, a soloist may sing it, or the choir may sing the stanza in English. Pronunciation guide is provided in "Teaching the Music." The congregation may join the choir in singing stanza 2.

WORDS: Joseph Mohr, adapt. by Frederico Fliedner
MUSIC: Franz Gruber, arr. by Albert Zabel

be - lla, anun-cian - do al ni - ñi - to Je - sús,
Ho - ly in - fant, so ten - der and mild,
heaven - ly hosts __ sing Al - le - lu - ia!

bri - lla la es - tre - lla de
sleep __ in heav - en-ly
Christ __ the Sav - ior is

F   C   G7

paz, _____
peace, _____
born, _____

bri - lla la es - tre - lla de paz.
sleep __ in heav - en - ly peace.
Christ, __ the Sav - ior is

C   C/G   G7   C

1, 2

Father: As we leave this place, may we always remember the lesson of Las Posadas.

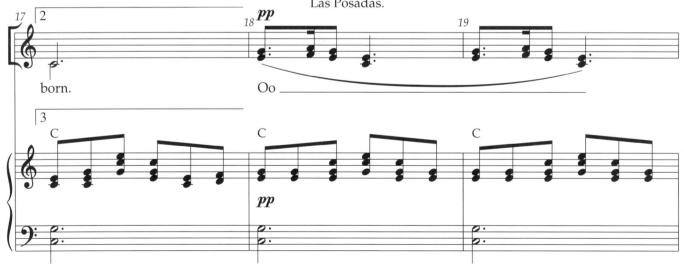

born.

pp

Oo _____

3

C   C   C

pp

Mother: May our homes be a haven for the poor and destitute…

Child 1: for the needy and the lonely.

Child 2: May we never turn away the homeless or the stranger.

Oo _____ Oo _____

Caroler 1: Jesus said that as we do to the less fortunate, so we do unto him.

Caroler 2: So, go in love and peace to serve all humanity.

Caroler 3: Amen and amen.

Oo _____ Christ, the Sav - ior, is born! _____

Christ, _ the Sav - ior, is born!

7. (Optional) Reprise:
Blessed Christmas Now Is Here

(Keyboard, opt. B♭ and C Instruments)

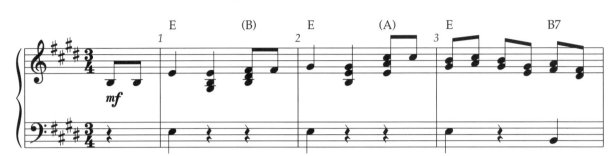

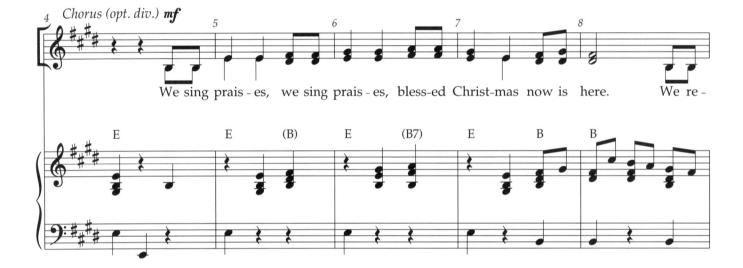

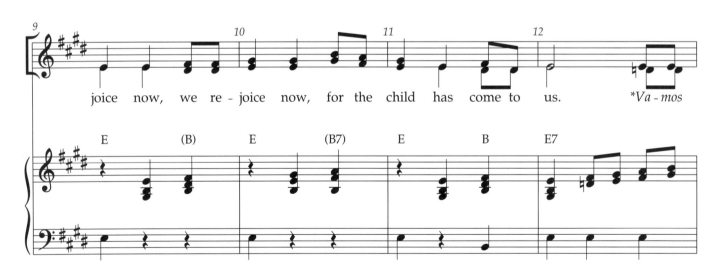

Pronunciation: vah-mos vah-mos ah es-pae-rahr-lo, vah-mos vah-mos ah bay-lin

Translation: Let's go, let's go wait for him, let's go to Bethlehem

WORDS: Trad. Argentina, trans. by Deborah Somuano
MUSIC: Trad. Argentina, arr. by Albert Zabel

1. Entrance Music

C Instruments

MUSIC: Trad. Argentina, arr. by Albert Zabel
© 2007 Abingdon Press, admin. by The Copyright Co., Nashville, TN 37212

2. Blessed Christmas Now Is Here

C Instruments

MUSIC: Trad. Argentina, arr. by Albert Zabel
© 2007 Abingdon Press, admin. by The Copyright Co., Nashville, TN 37212

3. Transition Music

C Instruments

MUSIC: Traditional, arr. by Albert Zabel

© 2007 Abingdon Press, admin. by The Copyright Co., Nashville, TN 37212

4. The Shepherds Go to Bethlehem

C Instruments

MUSIC: Traditional, arr. by Albert Zabel

5. Pidiendo Posada

C Instruments

MUSIC: Traditional, arr. by Albert Zabel

(optional repeat)

(optional repeat)

(optional repeat)

6. Silent Night!

¡Noche de paz!

C Instruments

MUSIC: Franz Gruber, arr. by Albert Zabel

© 2007 Abingdon Press, admin. by The Copyright Co., Nashville, TN 37212

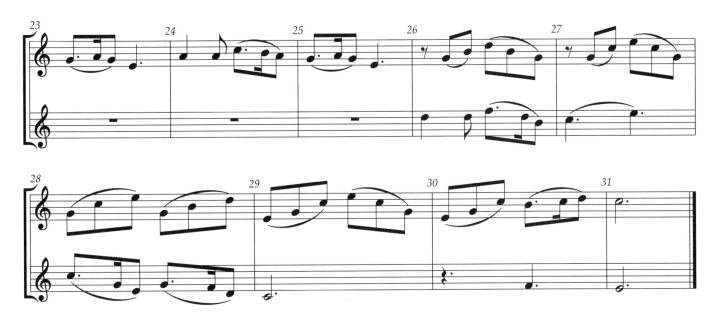

7. Optional Reprise:
Blessed Christmas Now is Here

C Instruments

MUSIC: Trad. Argentina, arr. by Albert Zabel

© 2007 Abingdon Press, admin. by The Copyright Co., Nashville, TN 37212

1. Entrance Music

B♭ Instruments

MUSIC: Trad. Argentina, arr. by Albert Zabel

© 2007 Abingdon Press, admin. by The Copyright Co., Nashville, TN 37212

2. Blessed Christmas Now Is Here

B♭ Instruments

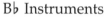

MUSIC: Trad. Argentina, arr. by Albert Zabel

© 2007 Abingdon Press, admin. by The Copyright Co., Nashville, TN 37212

3. Transition Music

Bb Instruments

MUSIC: Traditional, arr. by Albert Zabel

4. The Shepherds Go to Bethlehem

B♭ Instruments

5. Pidiendo Posada

B♭ Instruments

MUSIC: Traditional, arr. by Albert Zabel

© 2007 Abingdon Press, admin. by The Copyright Co., Nashville, TN 37212

6. Silent Night!
¡Noche de paz!

Bb Instruments

MUSIC: Franz Gruber, arr. by Albert Zabel

7. Optional Reprise:
Blessed Christmas Now Is Here

B♭ Instruments

MUSIC: Traditional, arr. by Albert Zabel

Singer's Book
Scene 1

*(Several **Carolers** and **Mrs. Morales** enter during Entrance Music.)*

Caroler 1:   Come on everyone. Let's get ourselves organized.

Caroler 2:   Do we have to go caroling when it's so cold?

Caroler 3:   Of course we do. Don't be so wimpy. We'll have a good time.

Caroler 4:   I wonder where Mrs. Romano is. We can't do our singing without a director.

Caroler 1 (6):   She must be running late.

Caroler 3 (7):   Look! There's a note on the table. *(Looks at it.)* It's from Mrs. Romano.

Caroler 1 (5):   Let me read it.

Caroler 2 (6):   *(Picks up note.)* I've got it.

Caroler 3 (7):   I found it, please let me read it.

(The note is handed to Caroler 3 [7] who reads the note while Caroler 2 [6] reads over their shoulder.)

Caroler 3 (7):   "Dear Children, I'm not feeling very well today. I won't be able to go caroling with you."

Caroler 4 (8):   *(Interrupting)* Oh no, that's bad news.

Caroler 3 (7):   *(Continuing to read.)* "Mrs. Morales will go caroling with you. Love, Mrs. Romano."

Caroler 2 (6):   Wait! There's more. "P.S. Be sure you practice the new Spanish carol before you leave."

Caroler 1:   But we can't practice without a director!

Caroler 3:   Mrs. Morales? Could you direct us?

Mrs. Morales: *(Sadly shakes her head "no.")* I don't know how to direct a choir.

Caroler 4:   What are we going to do?

Caroler 1 (5):   We still need a leader. How can we practice without a director?

Caroler 2:   I can do it. I can direct.

Caroler 4 (8):   No way!

Caroler 2:   Yes I can!

Caroler 4 (8):   This will be a disaster.

Caroler 3 (7):   At least let *him/her* try. That's what Mrs. Romano would want.

Caroler 1 (5): Well, since you put it that way. I guess something is better than nothing.

Caroler 2: Okay. Now everybody sing out, and watch me.

(**Carolers** *line up to sing as if in rehearsal.*)

2. Blessed Christmas Now Is Here

Chorus (opt. div.)

1. We sing prais - es, we sing prais - es, bless - ed
2. We will give him, we will give him, give our

Christ - mas now is here. We re - joice now, we re - joice now, for the
hearts un - to the Child. We will find him, we will find him, our sure

child has come to us. *Va - mos va - mos a es - pe - rar - lo, va - mos
hope and life is there.

va - mos a Be - lén, Our Lord Je - sus, in the man - ger, came to

set all peo - ple free. 2. We will

(mel. is bottom voice)

3. We will love him, we will love him for the les - son that he

Pronunciation: vah-mos vah-mos ah es-pae-rahr-lo, vah-mos vah-mos ah bay-lin
Translation: Let's go, let's go wait for him, let's go to Bethlehem
WORDS: Trad. Argentina, trans. by Deborah Somuano
MUSIC: Trad. Argentina, arr. by Albert Zabel

Scene 2

*(The scene opens on a living room with **Mother** and **Children** finishing decorating a Christmas tree. A Nativity set is prominently displayed. **Father** enters from the outside.)*

Father: Here are the rest of the decorations. Is it ever cold outside! And that wind—it chilled me to the bone.

Mother: Here, have something warm to drink. Remember those Christmases we had in Mexico? We never saw a bit of snow.

Child 1: I'll bet it wasn't very cold.

Child 2: I'm glad it's nice and warm in here.

Father: You're lucky you're not outside. Here, let me help you with that ornament.

Child 1: I can do it myself!

Father: Aren't you independent! You know, sometimes we do have to let others help us.

Child 2: May I put on the star?

*(**Carolers** are heard singing "Blessed Christmas Now Is Here" from offstage.)*

Mother: Of course. I think we're about done. Isn't it a pretty tree?

Father: Listen! There are some carolers outside. I saw them coming downt the street when I was outside.

*(**Children** look out the window.)*

Mother: Isn't that wonderful! Let's invite them in. They must be cold.

Child 1: No. Don't ask them in. They're strangers. We don't know them.

Child 2: I don't think they're from around here. They might be dangerous.

Child 1: Or different.

Father: Don't be silly. Where's your Christmas spirit? Mother, let them in.

*(**Mother** opens the door.)*

Mother: Come in! Come in! I'm sure you'd like to get out of the cold for a few minutes.

*(**Carolers** enter.)*

Father: Your singing was wonderful.

Caroler 4: We've been practicing very hard.

Caroler 2: Our director is very sick and couldn't come with us. I had to be the substitute director.

Mother: You're doing a fine job.

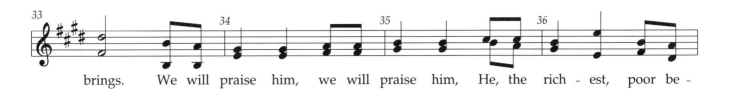

brings. We will praise him, we will praise him, He, the rich - est, poor be -

(mel. is top note)

came. Va - mos va - mos a es - pe - rar - lo, va - mos va - mos a Be -

(mel. is bottom note)

lén. Our Lord Je - sus, in the man - ger, came to set all peo - ple

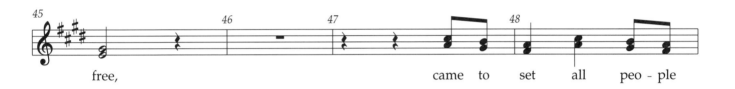

free, came to set all peo - ple

free, came to set all peo - ple free.

Caroler 2: Not bad. In fact, pretty good, if I do say so myself. I think I like this job.

Caroler 4: Don't get too excited. Remember, you're only a substitute.

Caroler 3: Come on. Stop fussing.

Caroler 1: I think we can do it!

Caroler 3 (7): Mrs. Morales, I'm glad you'll be with us.

Mrs. Morales: I'm glad to help out. I loved that song you were singing. I remember hearing my mother sing it.

Caroler 2 (6): Did you live in Mexico?

Mrs. Morales: Years ago when I was a child. Well, are you ready to go?

Caroler 2: We're ready. But, don't forget to watch me when we sing!

(Exit as the "Transition Music" plays.)

Caroler 1:	My mother came along to help out.
Mrs. Morales:	Good evening. I'm Anna Morales. Thank you for letting us come in. That cold is really wicked and we've come a long way.
Mother:	You're most welcome. Please make yourself at home.
Father:	We just finished decorating our tree and I was about to read the Christmas story from the Bible. It's something we do every year.
Mother:	Come join around our manger scene.
Child 1:	May I help read?
Child 2:	Me, too?
Father:	Of course. Perhaps some of our guests would like to read also. But let me begin. "In those days Caesar Augustus issued a decree that a census should be taken of the entire Roman world. This was the first census that took place while Quirinius was governor of Syria. And everyone went to his own town to register."
Child 1:	"So Joseph also went up from the town of Nazareth in Galilee to Judea, to Bethlehem, the town of David, because he belonged to the house and line of David. He went there to register with Mary, who was pledged to be married to him and was expecting a child."
Child 2:	"While they were there, the time came for the baby to be born, and she gave birth to her firstborn, a son. She wrapped him in cloths and placed him in a manger, because there was no room for them in the inn."
Caroler 1 (5):	"And there were shepherds living out in the fields nearby, keeping watch over their flocks at night. An angel of the Lord appeared to them, and the glory of the Lord shown around them, and they were terrified."
Caroler 4 (8):	"But the angel said to them, 'Do not be afraid. I bring you good news of great joy that will be for all the people. Today in the town of David a Savior has been born to you; he is Christ the Lord. This will be a sign to you: You will find a baby wrapped in cloths and lying in a manger'."
Child 2:	"Suddenly a great company of the heavenly host appeared with the angel, praising God and saying, 'Glory to God in the highest, and on earth, peace to men on whom his favor rests'."
Caroler 3 (4):	"When the angels had left them and gone into heaven, the shepherds said to one anther, 'Let's go to Bethlehem and see this thing that has happened, which the Lord has told us about'."
Mrs. Morales:	It's such a beautiful story.
Caroler 1:	I really love the part about the shepherds.
Mrs. Morales:	It reminds me of that carol I heard you practicing last week.
Caroler 3:	I know the one you mean. It's about the little shepherd that fell down and was left behind.
Mrs. Morales:	That's it! Would you sing it for us? I remember it from my childhood.

4. The Shepherds Go to Bethlehem

Optional: Soloist can sing stanza 1 and/or 2.

WORDS: Traditional, trans. by Deborah Somuano
MUSIC: Traditional, arr. by Albert Zabel

© 2007 Abingdon Press, admin. by The Copyright Co., Nashville, TN 37212

ay, we'll soon re - turn. Sing a tam, tam, tam, and a bou, bou, bou, sing a tam and a

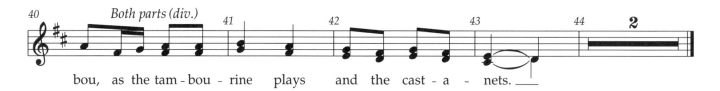

bou, as the tam - bou - rine plays and the cast - a - nets.

Mrs. Morales:	Thank you so much. That's such a happy piece and always one of my favorites.
Mother:	Let's finish the Bible story.
Caroler 2 (6):	"So they hurried off and found Mary and Joseph, and the baby, who was lying in the manger. When they had seen him, they spread the word concerning what had been told them about this child, and all who heard it were amazed at what the shepherds said to them."
Father:	"But Mary treasured up all these things and pondered them in her heart."
Child 1:	"The shepherds returned, glorifying and praising God for all the things they had heard and seen, which were just as they had been told."
Father:	What a wonderful story. I hope all of you will treasure it in your hearts as Mary did.
Mother:	Do you know, when we were your age, we lived in Mexico. At each year we had a celebration at Christmas called Las Posadas.
Caroler 1:	Las Posadas?
Caroler 3:	What was it about?
Mother:	It was about a part of the Christmas story you just heard.
Caroler 4:	About the shepherds?
Caroler 2:	Or the angels?
Father:	No. Remember what happened when Mary and Joseph reached Bethlehem?
Child 1:	The baby was coming at any moment.
Child 2:	And they couldn't find a place to stay.
Father:	Right! Las Posadas tells the story of Joseph looking for a place where the baby could be born. Remember the story says, "there was no room for them in the inn." Inns are what we might call hotels today. I imagine they went to several of them, but they were always turned away.
Mother:	No one would even open the door for them.
Child 2:	Maybe they were afraid because Mary and Joseph came from another town.
Child 1:	They were strangers.

Child 2:   That's why we were a little afraid to let all of you in.

Father: I have an idea. I think we should celebrate our own Posada. We have enough people here.

All: Really?

Father: Sure. Let's set up some inns—here, here, and over there. Some of you can be innkeepers and two of you can be Mary and Joseph looking for a place to stay.

*(**Children** divide into groups. **Mother** hands them props to create doorways.)*

Father: Are you ready? Now there's a little tune we sing as we go from place to place. It's very easy and we can all join in. Innkeepers, take your places. Mary and Joseph ready? Okay. Here we go.

5. Pidiendo Posada

WORDS: Traditional, trans. by Deborah Somuano
MUSIC: Traditional, arr. by Albert Zabel

hum-ble, ver - y hum-ble, we _ of - fer it to you. Let us sing with joy - ful

voic - es, joy - ful voic - es, we are hon-ored on this night, for we have the ho - ly

fam - 'ly, ho - ly fam - 'ly, safe-ly shel - tered in our house. _____

Father:	So, at last Mary and Joseph found a place to stay.
Mother:	A place where the precious baby could be born safely.
Caroler 1:	It probably wasn't anything fancy.
Caroler 2:	They may have been as cold as we were when we came in.
Father:	Perhaps. But, what's the important lesson we can learn from the Las Posadas drama we just did?
Caroler 3:	I know. Never give up.
Caroler 4:	Or, keep on trying.
Mother:	Good ideas, but I think there's a lesson even more important.
Child 1:	Sometimes it's okay not to be afraid of strangers.
Child 2:	Sometimes strangers need help.
Caroler 3 (7):	And strangers can become neighbors and friends.
Mother:	Can anyone remember a Bible verse about neighbors?
Caroler 4 (8):	I know. Love your neighbor as yourself.
Father:	Good for you! Jesus taught us that everyone is our neighbor. Everyone is to be loved—even strangers.
Mother:	In the book of Matthew, Jesus says, "I was a stranger and you took me in."
Caroler 3:	Just like the last innkeeper took in Mary and Joseph.
Father:	That's called hospitality. It comes from the same word as hospital—a place where people are cared for and welcomed. It also means sharing the gifts that God has given us.
Mother:	I like to think back to that first Christmas so many years ago. It was such a silent and holy night. The most wonderful night that ever was.

6. Silent Night!
¡Noche de paz!

Father: As we leave this place, may we always remember the lesson of Las Posadas.

Mother: May our homes be a haven for the poor and destitute…

Child 1: for the needy and the lonely.

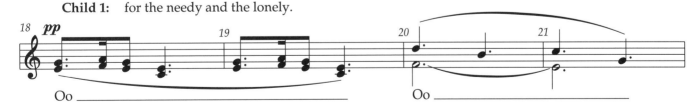

Options: The choir may sing the Spanish text, a soloist may sing it, or the choir may sing the stanze in English. Pronunciation guide is provided in "Teaching the Music." The congregation may join the choir in singing stanza 2.

WORDS: Joseph Mohr, adapt. by Frederico Fliedner
MUSIC: Franz Gruber, arr. by Albert Zabel

Child 2:   May we never turn away the homeless or the stranger.

Caroler 1:   Jesus said that as we do to the less fortunate, so we do unto him.

Caroler 2:   So, go in love and peace to serve all humanity.

Caroler 3:   Amen and amen.

Oo _____ Oo _____

Christ, the Sav-ior, is born! ____ Christ, _ the Sav-ior, is born!

7. Optional Reprise:
Blessed Christmas Now Is Here

We sing prais-es, we sing prais-es, bless-ed

Christ-mas now is here. We re-joice now, we re-joice now, for the child has come to

us. *Va-mos va-mos a es-pe-rar-lo, va-mos va-mos a Be-lén, Our Lord

Je-sus, in the man-ger, came to set all peo-ple free, came to

set all peo-ple free, came to set all peo-ple free.

Pronunciation: vah-mos vah-mos ah es-pae-rahr-lo, vah-mos vah-mos ah bay-lin
Translation: Let's go, let's go wait for him, let's go to Bethlehem

WORDS: Trad. Argentina, trans. by Deborah Somuano
MUSIC: Trad. Argentina, arr. by Albert Zabel

Las Posadas Resources

Books
- *The Night of Las Posadas.* Tomie dePaola (Putnam Juvenile, 1999, ISBN 0-3992-3400-40).
- *Las Posadas, An Hispanic Christmas Celebration.* Diane Hoyt-Goldsmith (Holiday House, 1999, ISBN 0-8234-1635-6).

Local Resources
- Contact your local Hispanic Chamber of Commerce, or other Hispanic community group for names of persons who can come and share stories of their celebration of Las Posadas.
- Watch for Las Posadas celebrations in your community. Plan a field trip with your choir!

Websites (correct as of print date)
- You will find many websites with information about Las Posadas by doing a search using the words "Las Posadas."
- http://www.sowingseeds.tv/ep11_posada.jsp
- http://www.pbase.com/davewyman/lasposadas
- http://www.scu.edu/diversity/poadas.html
- http://olvera-street.com/html/las_posadas.html
- http://www.ehow.com/how_7720_stage-las-posadas.html
- http://www.ehow.com/how_11722_celebrate-mexican-christmas.html

---

Track List

1. Entrance Music (#1)
2. Scene 1
3. Blessed Christmas Now Is Here (#2)
4. Scene 1, continued
5. Transition Music (#3)
6. Scene 2
7. The Shepherds Go to Bethlehem (#4)*
8. Scene 2, continued
9. Pidiendo Posada (#5)
10. Scene 2, continued
11. Silent Night (¡Noche de paz!) (#6)
12. Reprise: Blessed Christmas Now Is Here (#7)

Track nos. 3, 7, 9, 11, and 12 are split-track format.

(Note: Tambourine and castenets were intentionally not recorded so you can add them ad lib when using the track.)